MW01519138

APRèS SaTIE - FoR TWO AND FOUR HaNDS

APRÈS SATIE

FOR TWO &
FOUR HANDS

DEAN STEADMAN

Brick Books

Library and Archives Canada Cataloguing in Publication

Steadman, Dean, 1950–, author
        Après Satie : for two and four hands / Dean Steadman.

Poems.
Issued in print and electronic formats.
ISBN 978-1-77131-436-7 (paperback).—ISBN 978-1-77131-438-1 (pdf).—
ISBN 978-1-77131-437-4 (epub)

        I. Title.

PS8637.T38A77 2016   C811'.6   C2015-907889-X
                                                                   C2015-907890-3

Copyright © Dean Steadman, 2016

We acknowledge the Canada Council for the Arts, the Government of Canada
through the Canada Book Fund, and the Ontario Arts Council for their support of
our publishing program.

The book is set in Sabon.
The cover photograph is by Marijke Friesen.
Design and layout by Marijke Friesen.
Printed and bound by Sunville Printco Inc.

Brick Books
431 Boler Road, Box 20081
London, Ontario N6K 4G6

www.brickbooks.ca

For Boone, who fell from a great height a long way down, through my many hands and changing hearts, and disappeared. Disparu.

A work is created "artistically" so that its perception is impeded and the greatest possible effect is produced through the slowness of the perception. As a result of this lingering, the object is perceived not in its extension in space, but, so to speak, in its continuity.

—Viktor Shklovsky

J'aimerais jouer avec un piano qui aurait une grosse queue.

—Erik Satie

CONTENTS

"Bonjour Biqui, Bonjour!"
—a song fragment with a portrait of Suzanne Valadon
by Erik Satie, April 2, 1893

Theme and Vexations

[*D'une manière particulière*]
Aging and impecunious, the Velvet Gentleman replays
the melody of too few afternoons spent sailing toy boats
on the pond of the Luxembourg Gardens with Valadon
when she was "Biqui," a wave spilling through him, chromatic
and unrelieved, a theme he nurtured, charmed by her tender
little belch but vexed by the poses, painters, and ateliers,
her comely figure a model inspiring art in others but leaving
him impossibly alone, exposed without a tonal centre
before the fanfare for the big fat king of the monkeys
and the distillation of his thirst for shirt collars, handkerchiefs,
and umbrellas, when all he had of his own was furniture music
and an impulse to abstraction that he wrote into a song fragment
on Easter Sunday, a one-page manuscript in pen and ink,
adorned with an "authentic portrait," and titled, denying adieu,
Bonjour Biqui, Bonjour!

FANFaRE FOR THE BIG FAT KING
OF THE MONKeYS

Prélude de La Porte héroïque du ciel

Primo

[*Calme et profondément doux*]
       A heavy-set man, middle-aged, standing on the pages
of a hardcover book opened to the middle, floats above the Masonic
rooftops and smokeless chimneys of the nearby academy. His hands
are folded together at the second button of a well-tailored suit jacket.
His pressed pants flutter in the gentle uplift of morning air, and
a brown derby hat, neatly brushed, rests on a head of finely combed
hair. He looks as if he could be on his way to lecture a class
in aerodynamics or geophysics, but these are subjects he knows
nothing about. The truth is he has just read that the last mating pair
of a variety of orange weavers, songbirds with brilliant trilling voices,
has died in captivity, and he is contemplating grief in the absence
of song.

The Parable of Worms (*Vers de terre*)

Secondo

[*Avec sourdine*]
The gods at first gave him everything he aspired to, and more,
then withdrew his ability to enjoy the pleasures of his dreams.
This taught him humility, and thereafter he endured, a modest man,
possessed of only two desires:

      1) to kill all the gods, and
      2) to be the whirring vibrato of the bee's scented wings.

Underlying both desires, buried beneath a lifetime of dead skin cells,
nail clippings and hair loss, was a primal urge to be the sound of a worm,
that final symphonic intimacy, experienced but never heard by humankind
or fallen trees alike.

En Habit de cheval

Primo

[*Léger comme un oeuf*]

A beautiful woman, with a figure so slight she could be carried on the wind,
sleeps through her morning alarm, then wakes to find her lover gone
and an envelope addressed to her on his pillow. She opens the envelope
and reads that a beautiful woman, with a figure so slight she could be carried
on the wind, sleeps through her morning alarm, then wakes to find her lover
gone and an envelope addressed to her on his pillow. She laughs, clutching
the covers to her chin. *Such a clever young man*, she thinks. *And a stallion
in bed. His seed could sire champion show hunters*. But this is really of no
importance to her. While she thrills to the fashion of the mount – saddlery,
crops, breeches – her plan is to win the heart of a local widower whose wispy
white hair resembles the head of a late-summer dandelion nodding in the early
evening breeze.

La Chasse

Secondo

[*Naturellement*]
The mounted huntress
    knows the sounds
        of leaf and dale,

her swift, lean hounds.
    She knows as well
        where the hart abound

and at full gallop
    crosses the ground
        to let fly her fletcher's

fleet dart, its tip piercing
    the hearts of the hunted
        and mounted huntress.

Poudre d'or

[*Doux et calme*]

      A couple walk home arm in arm from church, the same church where over sixty years ago they were married. Her breasts and hips have ballooned with the passage of time, and he sports a belly bulging so large he cannot see the toes of his shoes. A pale full moon lingers in the morning sky above them. *Don't you wish the stars were visible during the day?* she asks. He has been too preoccupied with his footing to notice the moon and, unsure of the reason for his wife's question, simply pats her arm in reply. But her thoughts have already wandered to a memory of their first year of marriage and her first pregnancy.
So much had happened in so short a time that she felt set adrift in space. Her husband was sympathetic and tried everything he could to cheer her. One night, with water pastels, he painted a celestial map on her swollen abdomen. He coloured her protruding navel bright yellow to represent the hub of sun, then positioned each planet in orbit above the dark nebula of her pubic hair and below the Milky Way of her breasts.
The gesture comforted her and she was beginning to feel strong again when, some weeks later, she miscarried and spiralled into a depression where she would have remained had it not been for her husband's love and the compassion of family and friends. *I don't know, dear,* her husband says, picking up the thread of her question, *There's already so much right under my nose that I don't see.* She gently pats his arm, acknowledging his predicament, and they continue steadily along the narrow sidewalk like large, heavenly bodies across the night sky, trailing convections of fire and ice like confetti in their wake.

Mother's Day

Secondo

[*De très loin*]
Morning's a knit of daylight hours and dishes soaking.
And summer's a nesting vole. The kitchen's the only room
where the sun's slow to burst. Or the garden corner,
before the first rays burrow.
She thinks to plant the red azalea, a gift,
like a recovered memory, and drops a stitch,
unravelling the outstretched arms of a four-year-old,
ear-cupped and goggled, storming the dandelions
in the backyard, a parachute drop of silken seed.
Circling to land, he collapses on her lap in laughter,
a dizzying weave of earth and sky, sky and earth.
Her skeins of wool roll among the jams
and jellies, as she slips into a morning sleep, hands folded
in the reeds and rushes of her printed apron, her dreams
a cross-step waltz of geese in scarves, sparrows in sweaters,
the missing handles of teacups.

Parade

Primo

[*Expressif*]
A cleansing rain. Torrential. Flooding the town and surrounding areas
for weeks until finally the sun rises and the earth, refreshed, begins to suck
up the water in large belching quaffs. Also from the east comes a circus
caravan led by a ringmaster of renown, his moustachio ends waxed into
permanent exclamations, perfectly rounded o's. *CHARLES LE MAGNE!
MONSIEUR LOYAL!* Beside him on the bench seat of his extravagantly
painted wagon, his young daughter, a contortionist, perches on her forearms,
slight buttocks resting on her head, slender legs extended forward like
antennae. She appears to be mesmerized by the steady motion of the draft
horses, her eyes fixed on the flexing rhythm of their muscular flanks and
the pendular swing of their scrotums. She is thinking of the circus strongman
whose love has proven inconstant. The road ahead is lined with townsfolk,
cameras loaded and poised, necks craning for a first glimpse of the costumed
performers and the cages of exotic animals. *Smile, Piccolo!* the ringmaster
roars, standing up to crack his bullwhip over the heads of the plodding horses,
It's showtime!

The Protocol of Curtsy in the Soviet d'Arcueil

Secondo

[*La main très abaissée*]
It's a rat's tune, childlike in its tender irony and timid styling.
Born of the cataclysmic events of world wars, it sways uneasily
in the mysterious presence of Our Lady of Lowliness.

Still, there's something communal in how it leans into the abstract
dimensions of music and holds, like the impulse of verse,
to a different order of reality, discontinuous and disturbing,
inviting the listener to reconstruct the composer's original perceptions:

See the Little American Girl
in her navy blue sailor jacket, pleated white skirt, and knee stockings.
See her curtsy and hear the stowaway rats squeal with applause.

Now listen to the forlorn blasts
of the foghorn as her tiny steamboat disappears into the stormy sea,
and watch, yes, watch, if you can, as the child herself sinks,
sinks,
sinks,
below the waves,
her eyes and lips forming surprisingly perfect *o*'s.

When you introduce me
to the foreign Defence Minister's wife, fashionable in her pearls
and floor-length furs, say I greet her, my belly to the ground,
the unpaid piper of Arcueil.

Trois Morceaux en forme de poire

Primo

[*Munissez-vous de clairvoyance*]

    I posed for him on a number of occasions. He respected his models and was very serious about his work, although I can't say that I really cared for his paintings. Too Cubist for my taste. A boob where a knee should be. Three asses. That sort of thing. Not exactly the figure a girl hopes to cut in a man's imagination. Often he would recite poetry while painting. Poems he had written himself. I remember a few were quite good, but most were dreary, confessional pieces. Self-pitying, I thought. Then one day he whispered into my ear, *Le "je," ce n'est pas moi.* I forget who he was quoting. A French Symbolist, I think he said. But it wasn't the meaning of his words that affected me at the time. It was their vibration finding passage in my body, an accidental intimacy that deafened me until later that afternoon he closed the studio door behind me, the deadbolt slid into place, and I stepped alone out into the rush of evening traffic.

Dream Studies in Chinoiserie

Secondo

[*En y regardant à deux fois*]
Flight is common in depictions of the afterlife.
A crane rides a tortoise into eternity.

In her dream she knows the five-clawed dragon
signifies strength and authority.

Not all dreams heal. The pen is above all else.
Brushes, ink cakes, ink stones, and paper –

the four treasures of the scholar's studio.
She passes a monastery courtyard, hears

priests and scholars in conversation,
then spends the rest of the day doing

nothing. Harmony is not to criticize.
In her dream there is a boy with a drum,

a scholar waiting to receive the "hat and belt"
of government office, and a pilgrim posing

for a potter's moon flask. A pelican, in her piety,
feeds her starving young with drops of blood.

Musiques intimes et secrètes

Primo

[*Soigneusement et avec lenteur*]
Holding a small bouquet of violets, a nine-year-old girl stands beneath
a black umbrella in the square outside the village church. It is not
raining. The umbrella is for protection against falling stars, an event
she believes to be a nightly phenomenon. It will soon be daylight,
the church bell having just now tolled for Morning Prayer. Her neatly
parted hair is tied tightly back with a black satin ribbon that drapes onto
the nape of her neck. She is visualizing the sheet music of her favourite
hymn, entranced by the white spaces between the words, how the voice
they withhold is perfectly pitched to the silence of the un-notated music
flowing between the printed notes. She is practicing a piece she will sing
later this morning at her mother's funeral. The cobblestones are cold
beneath her feet, a damp cold that makes her regret not wearing the anklets
she had set out with her best blouse and tunic. Her mother's lace-cuffed
anklets. White as the moon. *La lune.* But not as white, she thinks,
as her mother's skin. Even her lips having paled.

Sunday Visit

Secondo

[*Sec comme un coucou*]
        Your grandmother dying
is the white of flour measured in thermos tops,
her heart a pounding waltz of bush elephants,
her soul a nosegay of ticket stubs ready to hand.

Words collide and crowd her room, a zoo
of pressed faces, ironed and starched,
your family articulate six ways to Sunday,
their constant chatter scrubbed and masked

by the prevailing din of help and hospice.
Words are such little monkeys, I hear her think.
But the poor dears are out of their tree here,
I'm afraid. Then her eyes finding my eyes pause,

bemused by my unfamiliar presence and awkward
silence but pleased to offer a matriarch's welcome:
Lumbering beasts, this herd. And melancholy mad.
It's our great ears, you see. Perfectly senseless!

Avant-dernières pensées

Primo

[*Portez cela plus loin*]

      She was singing a rondeau and pruning her centifolias
when a small bird, smaller than a hummingbird, flew into
her mouth and nested in her heart. She was not alarmed
by the incident, preoccupied as she was with preparations
for her lead role in *Djamileh*, and gave the matter little thought.
The opera was in the final week of rehearsals and the director,
though he had for years admired his diva's talents, was amazed
by how her voice seemed in recent days to have surpassed
its established excellence. The entire cast was likewise inspired
by the emotional range of her performance. On opening night,
as the curtain rose for the first of her arias, she opened
her mouth and the small bird emerged, its wings resplendent
in the floodlights. The audience gasped, their lips rounding
into *ooh*s and *aah*s as, to their further amazement, another
small bird escaped her mouth, then another and another, until
seven perfectly plumed specimens of a species long believed
to be extinct were freely circling the domed ceiling of the opera
house. The audience rose to its feet, some throwing bouquets
of flowers, others shouting, *Bravo! Bravo!* releasing tears
of gratitude and delight. Then, one of the birds fell to the stage,
its brittle body shattering on impact. A terrible silence gripped
the audience as one by one all the other birds fell like the first
drops of rain spoiling a long-awaited May Day.

Argument by Design

Secondo

[*De même couleur*]
　　　And then there remained
her question about the moon. Why only one moon
when:

　　　1. other planets have several;
　　　2. there are oceans and tides aplenty; and
　　　3. the sky on a cloudless day clearly needs

the adornment of a pendant gem or other reflective
bauble so its admirers can all say, *Yes, yes, yes.*
On you the blue is equally beautiful.

TRuE FLABBY PRELUDES
(FOR A DoG)

Nouvelles Pièces froides

Primo

[*Ouvrez la tête*]
Every year on her birthday she captured a rush of wind in a jar and labelled
the jar with the date. It was a birthday tradition she had begun as a child,
a precocious three-year-old, intrigued by the idea that something invisible
could be heard and deeply felt. Shelved neatly in chronological order,
the jars now numbered seventy-five and, as her birthday was in late December,
it was certain that if the winds were ever released, they would blow strong and
polar cold. Each jar displayed a fall of snow, some nearing blizzard conditions,
individual flakes suspended in mid-air, their crystalline structures unmatchable
in radiance. One jar, by far her favourite, contained a honeybee, a victim
of miscalculation having awakened prematurely from its winter sleep.
Its silvery wings were frozen in motion, inseparable from the glitter, while,
stark against the blustery pale, its black and yellow stripes buzzed electric.

All Fall Down

Secondo

[*Le chant bien en dehors*]
The chiming of glass wind,
       ever-present, in-

visible, I thought as a child,
       the music elemental,

like light changing,
       subtle shades

of green, sky blue,
       intangible as air

before wind.
       Then to find

the tonal transparency
       suspended

by red silken threads.
       The glass rectangles spinning

real, and colliding,
       gentle as children

dizzy in play –
       husha husha we all –

or as death
       that fall day circling

my grandfather's bed,
       the coil around his voice,

rattling, delirious with fever,
husha husha.

Gymnopédie No. 1

[*Lent et douloureux*]

The night I came to meet you at the Gare Montparnasse, all the trains
were running late and the platforms were filled with tired, impatient
travellers. We stopped for a minute outside the station to catch our breath
and listen to a busker's solo violin, and when I reached down to pick up
your valise it was gone. The only clothes you had for the weekend were
those you were wearing and they hung in the bedroom closet until Monday
morning when we woke to the clock radio playing a piano composition
you once admired, a piece you had danced to at the Palais Garnier. But
that morning the music made you sad and you dressed in the half-light
leaving your nakedness on the hanger where over the next week it faded
away, except for the impression of a row of buttons down your back.

Pages mystiques

Primo

[*Dans la plus profonde silence*]
Lost in an epic novel, a minor character uses lines of the text to climb
to the top of a page. There, perching precariously on the page number,
he looks out for the first time on the external world as the sun rises.
He is alarmed by the blinding splendour and the warmth on his face.
He has only ever experienced sun in black and white. Now the noises
and smells waking around him in forest greens and tempered blues
are so overwhelming that he teeters and loses his balance. He falls
to the foot of the page in a heap of punctuation and dislodged letters.
Rising to his feet with the help of an exclamation mark, he exclaims,
I am singular, sent by the sun! Unimpressed, his fellow characters
sigh their disapproval, dismissing his outrageous outburst as an all-
too-common display of the fragmented psyche's isolation and grief.

Leaving Eden

Secondo

[*Lent et détaché sans sécheresse*]
Can an agonized expression really conceal pleasure,
or is the pain of loving a constant pushing in or away,
bruising the body like fallen fruit, our seed exposed to soil?
Are the lyrics *She loves you yeah yeah yeah* tattooed
above her breasts intended to convey passion or hostility?
How did she learn to be so naked in the first place?
Is most sex funny, Henri Bergson funny, the body failing
to perform up to the standards of the spirit,
the material world resisting the impulses of the will?
Is her tenderness sincere or rehearsed, is it just ourselves
we see in those we think we love? Coupled with me
does she feel godlike and helpless all at once,
or just cacophonous and unclothed, ashamed of exile
in a world with edges, and oh so tired of my touch?

Sonatine bureaucratique

Primo

[*Comme une bête*]

A young bureaucrat falls in love with the beautiful circus contortionist.
They marry. But she quickly tires of him and runs off with the strongman,
leaving the hapless bureaucrat heartbroken. He spirals into depression,
some days never leaves his bed. At night his dreams begin to fill
with terrifying images that spill over into morning. One night he dreams
he is a circus bear and wakes to find the dead body of a trained seal
in his bed. In panic, he wraps the seal in a sheet and carries it
to his local butcher who eyes him with suspicion but accepts the animal,
realizing the potential profit in sales of choice cuts. Then he dreams
he is a parading elephant and wakes to find the trodden body of a zebra
beside his bed. The creature is too big to move alone so he calls Star Top
Cartage Co. Two burly men appear at his door and, after some hesitation,
accept the job, knowing that the hide alone will fetch a pretty penny
for the morning's work. Such dreams, involving a full menagerie of circus
animals, continue for weeks. Then one night, the young man does not
dream at all. In the morning when he opens his eyes, there is only a spot-lit
patch of sunlight on his bedroom floor. Confident that his former self
has been restored, he weeps tears of joy and steps like a ringmaster into
the brilliance of the light to take a deep, appreciative bow, unaware
of the big cats moving into position behind him.

On Formally Undecidable Propositions
and the Arithmetic of Whole Numbers

Secondo

[*Positivement*]
A world view so stellar in its appeal
you'd think it would have gathered
a magi following by now. But no,
it seems there will always be a need
to prove the need for a better mouse trap.
(No, sorry, that's not it. Let me start again.)
There will always be ~~an England~~ a need
for a Gödel (your patience, please!) to prove
even the most basic axioms of arithmetic
cannot be proved or disproved, leaving
young love reason to believe one plus one
(or, in the parlance of dance, *cha-cha-cha*)
is one, only more whole and one-drous.

Croquis et agaceries d'un gros bonhomme en bois

Primo

[*Plein de subtilité, si vous m'en croyez*]
Paint it and they will come, the real estate agent suggests. *And buy?* I ask.
Okay, bye for now, she says hanging up. *Don't . . . merde!* I sputter,
staring dumbfounded at the phone before slamming it back into its cradle.
Can't we just bake bread? I yell at my wife, soon-to-be ex, who looks up
bemused and frightened, the dinner plate in her hand suspended above
a half-packed moving box. *Isn't that what couples like us do to hide
the ghost rectangles and squares haunting the walls. Let the new owners –*
Assez, assez! she interrupts, tears swelling in her eyes as she screams, *Look
at the way we loved, sniffing each other for the best-before date.* And that,
mon ami, is the straw that breaks the camel's balls, my mind now racing
even faster averaging the legal fees by the number of rooms that will never
echo with the sound of front steps being shovelled in winter or lawns being
raked in summer more like unfamiliar dogs now that you mention tracking
God knows through each open-house be it never so humbled and the agent
channelling Doris Day with her wholesome sweet looks and good house-
keeping smile of approval while none of us realizes that every fucking prospect
is tanking because of the pristine primaries and untarnished domesticity
of the backyard swing set and jungle gym overlooked by our hurry-up-happy
movers but seen as a harbinger of heartbreak by the starter-home set who
would prefer a basement of gators to a single snake in the garden.

URs truly,

Secondo

[*Allez modérément*]
After he croaked (self-croaked), an ex blabbed
he'd hated himself. Said he'd detested his music,
abhorred his ardent admirers' vinyl ears.
That's right, Buttercup. *Il vous haïssait à mort.*
Not you personally. (*Bien sûr, chérie,* he'd have wetted
himself.) The herd you. The ewe even u despise
and keep caged in ur wallet (nm *portefeuille*) for ID
(e.g., *qui suis-je?*)

P.S.

Q.   Which pose would best express the transformation
of JC from human to divine?

A.   a)   nm *profil,*
b)   headstand,
c)   ½ lotus,
xoxo)   romantic irony.

Trois Gnossiennes

Primo

[*Avec conviction et avec une tristesse rigoureuse*]
The night I performed as a maiden in the crane dance outside the entrance
to the cypress maze at the Grand Duke's Chateau Knossos, I fell in love
with a beast of a man, bullish and brutal, who could love me only physically,
a limitation not without its pleasures and one I welcomed until the day,
while rehearsing a sarabande, I became entranced by my reflection
in the mirrored walls of the studio and realized for the first time that I liked
who I was seeing, her long legs, slender torso, and regal neck, the fact that,
even flightless, she had the grace of an egret or sacred ibis and the ability
to slip though the cypress needles to solve the mystery of the labyrinth and slay
the Minotaur without weakening at the shocked look of betrayal in his eyes,
though never forgetting how he once spilled himself onto my body.

Authentic Portrait

Secondo

[*Pliez-vous soigneusement*]
A black and white still
      with asphodels
            and scalloped edges
Your ten tiptoes
      hand-tinted red
         your mouth
           o
circling back, arched
        and laughing
the perfect solar
     crescent
        of eclipse

Gymnopédie No. 2

[*Plein de subtilité, si vous m'en croyez*]

        The audition for the season's sarabande was your last.
The music hung from your body like a borrowed winter coat, heavy
and oversized. Then the mishap of miscue, misstep, and tumble.
And afterwards walking all the way to our old address in Montparnasse
to find the building semi-demolished, the shell of bricks and mortar
hammered away, exposing a skeletal framework that your eyes climbed
floor by floor to the top apartment, wondering if it had been emptied
thoroughly, the drawers and closets checked for anything overlooked
or forgotten, something possibly invisible.

Sur une lanterne

Primo

[*Bêtement et lourdement*]

A young girl, mistakable for Degas' Little Dancer, leads a mare along
a fog-filled road and passes a weeping man carrying a suitcase, walking
in the opposite direction. The road is lit by the yellow haze of moonlight.
Overhead in the darkness are flocks of migratory marsh birds navigating
by instinct. The man is on his way to the bedside of a dying friend.
The girl has no idea where she is going but is certain she will never
travel this road again. She regrets that in her haste she has left behind
a set of glass buttons given to her by her mother. Her sadness is obvious
to the man with the suitcase, but it is only as she passes that he notices
the mare's eyes are blind.

Flight of the Luna Moth

Secondo

[*Montez sur vos doigts*]
      She wore an egret feather
in her hat's tether and thought it
      bold, stylish, à la mode,
akin to body piercing or other forms
of aesthetic disfigurement
      that, truth be told,
            she didn't much care
               for, but still
she persisted, flying into the wind
with a maddish grin, taking refuge
      in trees, finding sanctuary
         under leaves,
           and there
imagining the pupa's fright awakening
one night not a butterfly.

Première pensée Rose + Croix

Primo

[*Mélancolique*]

An old man, a pensioner, dials his insurance company to report his wife's death. The call is redirected to a claims agent who asks the cause of death. The man thinks to say *life* but instead says, *She stopped breathing.* The agent hesitates before continuing, *I see, sir. I know this must be difficult for you. I'll put "heart failure."* No, *no,* the husband says, *That wasn't it. That wasn't it at all. We loved each other until the very end.* Another long silence. *Of course, sir,* the agent says, *I'll just write "unknown" and ask that the file be given priority. There's no rush,* says the old man, hanging up, unsure why he'd phoned in the first place, wondering if it was something on the to-do list he'd had nothing to do with, a list handwritten in a wave of perfect cursive, each letter cresting into the next or breaking unpronounced into the space between the words.

Sea Change

Secondo

[*Des 2 mains*]
The waves unroll their agency
in turns of ebb
                    and flow,
the surf washing over the ribbed
wreckage   channelling
some little salvage back
to the primal cunt of sanctuary,
before the piracy of egg,
the plunder of womb.

Un Dîner à l'Élysée

[*En blanc et immobile*]

A curious girl in search of the alchemy of honey one day
disturbs a hive of bees and is stung numerous times. She suffers
a rare reaction, nearly fatal, her brain swelling and robbing her
of many basic cognitive skills. Several years pass and her widowed
mother dies during an outbreak of influenza, leaving the girl, now
a young woman, on her own. She has no concept of death and
spends her days in the village square waiting for her mother's return.
She examines every face that passes by but, of course, none is ever
that of her departed mother. Touched by her loss, the villagers
begin to give her small gifts of food and clothing. One market day,
the son of a local apiarist enters the village with a cartload of potted
honey and waxy blocks of comb. He sees the other vendors leaving
the young woman samplings of their produce and decides to do
likewise. He hands her a pot of prize clover honey and she gives
him a friendly kiss on the cheek in return, his beard stubble prickling,
almost stinging her lips. The sensation rouses a dormant curiosity
that makes her slow to withdraw from the scent of nectar on his skin
and the murmured whir of his busy heart.

La Diva de l'Empire

Primo

[*Conseillez-vous soigneusement*]
He was seventy-seven years old when a Breton folk dance stepped
its way into his heart at the spring fair, in large measure owing
to the accomplished performance of a young village beauty. Wide-
hipped and heavy-breasted she was and, sadly for our sorry fellow,
she never once noticed his enamoured gaze among the faces
of the elderly attending the day's events. Her eyes were busy
searching the crowd for a blond, tuft-haired boy whose gangly arms
and legs lent him an awkward charm. He was nowhere to be seen,
however, having found day-work as a labourer with the circus
that toured the region each year as part of the vernal celebrations.
There, under the big top, he was attracted to the ringmaster's daughter,
a slimly built contortionist. One night after the crowds had dispersed
and with the circus bedded down, she entertained the tufted one
with her "Portal to Venus" pose, one she performed only for her most
select admirers. In that moment, the youth transcended his lanky
earthbound form, finding the far reaches of the universe in the arms
of the carnal contortionist. There he dreamt of two-stepping in time
with a certain village beauty who he believed had eyes only for him.
But when next morning he awoke, the circus had moved on and
the girl of his dreams had eyes for another.

Morning Shades an Evening Hue

Secondo

[*De moitié premier temps*]
Full she was in flower
uprooted by the storm
petals rained down for hours
each hour an hour to mourn.

He saved all the petals
in caskets one, two, three
caskets of rare metals
and threaded filigree.

These he placed on a sill
to prosper in the sun
green stems began to spill
and flower one by one.

Each day new tendrils spread
their arms held open wide
and twined around their bed
with her entombed inside.

He then twice lit the vine
fanning the rosy flames
and pressed his lips to mine
his one love once again.

Gymnopédie No. 3

[*Sans bruit, croyez-moi encore*]

      Unpacking the bed linens, you find an envelope containing
twelve glass buttons, mementos of a dance costume long ago
misplaced. *Giselle's? Maybe,* you think, placing the buttons on
the windowsill where they refract the winter light into tiny spectra
on the bedroom walls. You smile to think how seldom you bother
with fasteners anymore, how you let drape your clothes over the life
growing within you as each day your once-slender torso expands
in rhythm with the arrival of spring, fairy godmother of the seasons.
That's it. Of course, Cinderella's ball gown! Scenes of a rehearsal
step through your mind. Directors huddled in the footlights, passionate
in debate. *The gown needs more sparkle. She must be radiant!*
You heard the magic in their enthusiasm and thrilled to the prospect
of a new gown. But the costume designer heard only dissatisfaction
and quit, disappeared from dance altogether, some said to pursue
her pastime as a small-scale producer of gourds, melons, and squashes.
Others said she became a beekeeper. Keeper of bees.

MeMOIRS OF AN
AMNESIaC

Messe des pauvres

Primus

[*Avec un grand oubli du present*]

A young woman,
not yet twenty, eyes the blue of Saharan sky, leaves the travelling
circus owned and operated by her parents to study dance in Paris.
Her father, a former commander with a French colonial unit
in northern Africa, mourns her departure but gladly enough funds
her ambitions. Her mother is also saddened by the loss of her only
child but, having herself lost her youth to a childhood of poverty
in her native Tunisia, is happy to see her daughter's storybook life
unfold. The first nights away from home are spent in an inexpensive
but comfortable hotel, and soon she finds a small apartment near
the academy in the shadow of Sacré-Coeur, the sculpted cloud atop
Montmartre. The week before classes start, she sleeps and dreams.
Mostly dreams. Of saints and martyrs, and of thieves stealing
into the vaults of her subconscious.

The Dismas Frescoes

Secondus

[*Même affirmation mais plus intérieure*]
I) **Negev**

We were thieves in the desert,
Preying on travellers and penitent Jews.
We descended on Carmen but she had no riches.

She bathed and anointed
Our feet with scented oils, prepared us teas
From the nectar and stamina of cactus flowers.

At sunrise, she left our camp.
Her shadow stretched out like a bridal train
Beyond the tents and onto the dunes.

We did not follow.
But in time we were drawn from the desert.
To Jerusalem. Like thorns from flesh.

✳

Carmen: If you live in the desert,
You become the sun. In Tunisia, where I was born,
There is an ancient word for this.

It is also the word for a colour.
It cracks in your mouth as you say it,
Like a bone breaking.

II) Jerusalem

We travelled by starlight
When the desert air was cool. Each night
The winds resculpted the dunes.

We stayed our course
And entered the city through the south gate
When the public fountain was awash in first light.

The women in the square
Eyed us with suspicion. Their tongues
Rattled with spit and secret discourse.

Some knew of Carmen,
Thought she had moved with others
To Bethany. *You'd be wise to follow*, they said.

Her sketches and paintings
Hung in halls we had marked for looting.
Her mosaics lit the places where we slept.

We found her in a hospice,
Pale among the dying. The matrons believed
We were kin and gave us her belongings.

✳

Entering the city was a mistake.
The authorities were onto us in days.
A Roman frenzy of arrests and crucifixions.

III) Golgotha

It was a circus,
A diversionary amusement. The soldiers broke
Our legs to speed on death.

Two thieves and a "Saviour,"
They called us. Gestas spat back but he too
Joined in goading the one they had crowned.

He was relentless
And together we fulfilled a prophecy.
I alone was promised paradise.

IV) The Place of the Skull

Dismas: What was the word
She saved? Do you remember, Gestas?
Among her colours. A word.

Gestas: There was no word.
There was never any word, Dismas.
You should know that. You were there.

As if he could ever forget
Carmen's ways, how she had shaped a world
Of promise in a single syllable.

I only wanted him to say it,
To help slake the thirst in his throat, dry
From the nightly sea-change of desert sand.

✲

Carmen's last possessions:
Burnt and raw sienna, carbon black, malachite,
Azurite, cinnabar; vermilion for skin tones;

The oldest known word,
Transcribed from a language of ancient nomads
In ink of cobalt blue, and wrapped in supple skins.

❋

We

A MAMMAL'S NOTeBOOK

Regret des Enfermés (Jonas and Latude)

Primo

[*Pas vite (rêvez doucement)*]
      In the Musée d'Orsay, the clouds in a Dufy landscape drift
from the painting across the gallery wall in search of an open window.
A young boy lets go of his mother's hand and follows the clouds into
the main corridor where he is nearly bowled over by a paint-smeared
smock running at full stride, the artist wrapped within shouting
profanities at the escaping clouds. The clouds gather speed, taking
on a stormy quality unfamiliar to the artist who now realizes they are
not his clouds after all. Returning to his easel, he stops to hand
the teary-eyed boy a jar of playing marbles and to apologize
to the tot's mother, a Spanish beauty, visibly upset, her slender fingers
ravelling a ringlet of hair. He is inspired by her glamorous tresses and,
fumbling, finds a carved ivory comb in an interior pocket of his smock.
He places it in the palm of her hand, gently closing her fingers overtop.
In return, she smiles, revealing the painter's elusive clouds adrift
in the blue depths of her eyes.

Cumulonimbus in E Minor

Secondo

[*Sans méchanceté*]
You seEminEminEminEminEminEminEminEminEminEminEminEminEmin
EminEminEminEminEminEminEminEminEminEminEminEminEmin
EminEminEminEminEminEminEminEminEminEminEminEmin
EminEminEminEminEminEminEminEminEminEminEmin
EminEminEminEminEminEminEminEminutes after
even a full day of rain
    the clouds would gather again
        like street toughs to rumble
and punch the sun's lights out.
    It was all kinda stupid tho
        cuz next they'd want to run
thru the park and splash
    their reflections in all the puddles.
        The nice green park with the benches.
But in the dark they couldn't see diddly.
    Dumb-ass clouds. And it's not like
        they didn't love the sun. They did.
They loved him above all elsEminEminEminEminEminEminEminEminEmin
EminEminEminEminEminEminEminEminEminEminEminEminEmin
EminEminEminEminEminEminEminEminEminEminEminEmin
and then somEminEminEminEminEminEminEminEminEmin . . .

It's just a lot of the time they disloved him even more.

Vieux sequins et vieilles cuirasses

[*Lent et avec précaution*]

From a distance, the two white-haired gentlemen in the park
appear to be waltzing with full-figured women, but closer
you observe that they are engaged in a game of chess, played
with human-size pieces they slide with little effort across
a checkered grid painted onto a portion of the paved area
surrounding a magnificent fountain. Antoine is eighty-eight
and Marcel is ninety-one. The two friends have met at chess
every Tuesday and Thursday afternoon for over twenty years.
Antoine has never won a game. He has come close and
a number of games have ended in stalemate, but he has never
managed to beat Marcel. This has attracted the wonder
of spectators, mostly widowed colleagues and acquaintances
who have come to attach a millennial significance to the possibility
of an Antoine victory. Today, a gull flying overhead splatters
the black crown of Antoine's queen, leaving her veiled
and saintly looking. Expectations of the onlookers immediately
run high in favour of Antoine, and even Antoine is so enthralled
by the transformation that he refuses to move the ebony Virgin
from her newly hallowed position, with the result that she and
the game are soon lost to the invincible Marcel.

Jeux de Gargantua (Coin de Polka)

Primo

[*De manière à obtenir un creux*]
Every harvest, Alphonse's grandfather toured the southern vineyards
with Toulouse, his beloved brown bear. Trained as a cub, Toulouse
had grown to a formidable weight and his massive hind paws
were skilled at straightening the knotted back muscles of the tawny
grape pickers. Part circus, part feast day, their annual visits marked
occasion for rest and merriment, with vineyard tables soon set with
linens and laden with cellared wines and local dishes, harvest fresh.
A master of ceremony, the old man knew to prolong the long-
awaited moment before gently bringing Toulouse to a standing
position and guiding him like a harnessed aerialist along the taut
spinal cord of a prostrate harvester. Quickly a circle of onlookers
would form, all laughing gaily as they waited their turn, the elderly
and arthritic offering silent prayers of gratitude for the miracle
of Saint Toulouse. The day Toulouse died, a dappled mare, blind
and unbridled, was sighted standing head down by the village railway
tracks. *Hope she's not waiting for the next train*, the villagers joked,
the trains having been rerouted years ago. No one claimed the poor
beast and so Alphonse's grandfather, feeling lonely for company
and with nothing to lose, fed it oats and apples and rode it bareback
home.

The Wedding Singer

Secondo

[*S'imbiber*]
Ancient cities are buried here, silted over and layered
like tiers of a wedding cake. Cut a little into the crusted

millennia and you'll find a sculpted Christ shaped into
the figure of a bridegroom. Slice deeper and treasure

the ruins of a people who worshipped the sun as a god.
And why not? When it was known to have bedded

all the emperors' radiant wives and would sing unabashedly
at their daughters' weddings, having ripened the grapes

of the best wines first so they could be enjoyed to the last.
Now cut to the core and witness the union of rock

and fire accompanied in song by a voice seminal to sound
but unborn to the human ear, its tenor so textured

could you hear it you'd stir nightly between your sheets
for a billion years aroused by its modulations.

Fête donnée par des Chevaliers Normands en l'Honneur d'une jeune Demoiselle (XIe siècle)

Primo

[*Beaucoup d'expression*]
She was thirteen and inspired by the lives of the canonized
sisters and martyrs when she swore a perpetual vow of chastity.
Then she began to have dreams containing images and events
outside the scope of her knowledge of past and present, so she
concluded that she must be dreaming the future. One dream
that recurred featured a young singer from America. Handsome
he was and provocative in ways she could not understand.
She had heard no other music than that sung by school or
church choirs, and those songs and hymns had never aroused
the sort of thoughts and feelings that she now experienced
in her dreams. She tried to describe the singer and his lyrical
gyrations to her music teacher, Sister Cecilia, who laughed
good-naturedly and hugged her tenderly, saying, *You truly
are a dreamer, dear one. Nothing of the kind exists, not even
in America!* And so the dreams continued unexplained
for several more years until one night in the arms of a young
soccer star from a neighbouring school, her dreams
of the future were lost forever, along with her vow of chastity.

Devotions of an American Beauty

Secondo

[*Vous pouvez allumer si vous voulez*]
Sure, go right ahead. Cut St. Audrey's cloth into virgin vows
and coronation garments. Let that Singer hum and sew up
a thousand tawdry frills. But it's got to end there, darlin'.
Don't you see? It's all for naught. Elvis don't love you tender.
He's hot for Ann-Margret. She's got the legs to dance
the sacrifice into heaven. She once wrapped them shapely gams
of hers around his neck and he went blind channelling the sun.
He's never going to marry you. Ask the Colonel. That's right.
Dial up Tom Parker. Or try to find the voice in the stereo cabinet.
Be Nipper, the RCA hound dog. Remaster the vacuum tubes
in the television set and commandeer The Ed Sullivan Show.
Now *that* would be sainthood enough. Better than martyrdom.
You wouldn't even have to bleed roses.

Désespoir agréable

Primo

[*Un peu vif*]
I tried so hard to get pregnant with my first husband that I'm sure
we set a fucking record. That's "fucking" as noun and I'm sorry
if it offends but there's no delicate way of putting this.
This wasn't about making love. It wasn't even about "having sex."
This was the baby business and we were ruthless CEOs prepared
to work every position in any room of the house at any hour
of the day. We ate, drank, and dreamt our obsession and fretted over
the fertile moments we were missing at our paying jobs, standing
in grocery lines, riding the metro. I tell you I saw more dick
in our first year of marriage than the Whore of Babylon did in all
of biblical history. And it didn't stop there. I thermometered, timed,
and calculated the movement of every egg my ovaries released.
I stood on my head after coitus. Come on! I bent over backwards.
Nothing. Not even an ectopic pregnancy. Mine was the Greenwich
Mean Time of monthly cycles. And what's more, we were both tested
by experts and identified as a potential population explosion.
I was Africa. He was Asia. Our tectonic plates were continually
colliding, grinding, and erupting into each other. It was a miracle
that he had even an inch of cock left after that year. But not the miracle
we needed to salvage our marriage. Then I met Tomás. I swear
all he did was look at me and I conceived. Well okay, we must have
shared the customary handshake. But really. It was that simple.
I'm just saying.

Sonnet Gestation

Secondo

[*Grossir*]
I
,

(a)m
I'
(a)m
'I
(a)m
,

I
(a)m
I
a)m
I
am

La Belle Excentrique, serious fantasy

Primo

[*Un peu mouvementé*]
A young woman, nearing full term, enters a bus shelter and hastens
to sit down on the pumpkin-coloured bench. *No time, Toulouse,*
she humours herself, *Don't dilly, Dali.* Closing her eyes, she imagines
being transported down the city's boulevards to the Seine and all
the pretty riverboats and barges. Her plan today is to cross from bank
to bank over as many bridges as possible, waving to the booksellers
along the way. The day passes quickly, and when the bridge lights
start to flicker so begins the return trip to her empty apartment.
The bus avoids the evening traffic by using the narrow side streets,
and slows as it approaches a sidewalk café where at a corner table
sits a solitary figure, *une belle dame d'une certaine âge.* Wearing
only a pair of black high-heeled shoes and a string of freshwater pearls,
she is elegantly naked. She sits with legs crossed, one shoe lazily
swinging from the tip of a toe, and holds a wine glass aloft, her elbow
resting on the arm of her chair. She waves to the young woman and
gestures toward an empty seat at her table. The young woman laughs,
tempted by the invitation. But it is late and she has been cautioned
not to overexert herself. Smiling, she shrugs and pats her protuberant
belly to signal her regrets. The bus carries on, past detritus of cinders
and slag in the factory district, finding its way onto the familiar streets
of her quartier. Tired from the day's outing, she stretches and,
reaching above her head to ring the bell for the next stop, releases
a tender little belch. *A slipper of the pregnant variety*, she muses
disembarking, pausing slightly on the final step to wave a *goodnight*
over her shoulder to no one in particular.

Paradise Found

Secondo

[*Munissez-vous de clairvoyance*]
Born into a late season's morning,
eyes December grey, the chilling cusp

of Capricorn, and your skin thinly
downed, translucent as fallen leaves

and, like their hollowed veins, exposed
to winter's laboured approach –

hunchbacked and heavy-footed,
snow-blind, dragging the dark

like a woven cloak. Yes, little one,
there were other mornings, other seasons.

But look at it this way – winter's only
summer sleeping. And besides,

doesn't this cycle of appear and disappear
make you smile, as if there could be

a playful God, and the day-to-night spin,
the windswept dance of a planet's tilted

orbit around a steadying star, a sort of tag,
a tireless game of hide-and-go-seek. And you,

familiar from birth with concealed shapes
and shadows, fiendishly clever at being "it."

De l'enfance de Pantagruel (Rêverie)

Primo

[*Comme un rossignol qui aurait mal aux dents*]
She could never recall how it was she swallowed the four
starling eggs she'd found one morning in the flowering
acacia tree in her backyard. But swallow them she did
and soon after gave birth to four burly boys. Their bodies
were thickly haired and robustly limbed, not at all feathered
or starling-winged. Three of the lads grew to be giants,
these being ancient times, while the fourth became a god
who lived an eternity in a state of unrequited love before
hanging himself in an ungodly manner. *Quelle catastrophe!*
his fellow gods jested. *Who'd have thought the old poof
so well-hung.* The giants attended their brother's funeral
and then travelled a long distance to tell their mother
the dark news. She was grief-stricken and further saddened
when the three lumbered away, now too large to enter
their childhood home. Her sorrow was more than she could
bear alone and, in a fit of despair, she felled the acacia tree
that for years had flowered in her backyard. It left a space
the same shape as the tree that during the day filled with
the passing profiles of migratory birds, and, at night, with
the wind-borne blossoms of neighbouring trees.

A Brief History of Round-Trip Travel

Secondo

[*Hors la tête*]
BECAUSE THEY WERE GIANTS (and could)
they rolled the clouds into huge white balls,
like children building snowmen,
and with their icy hands polished the rings
they'd made around this little *o* of earth
until they shone like wedding bands.

This aroused ringed-Saturn's timeless ire
and sneering his disdain with sickle-thin lips
he denounced the vanity of GIANT wishes,
his elocution lost on wingless Cupid
who, trapped in the Time god's allegory,
found inspiration in the GIANT's ringed spectacle

and, in a fit of fancy, entertained visions of travelling
big tops and barking seals, acrobatic dwarves,
fire-eaters balanced on prancing ponies, and Fat Ladies
with tattoos in places Strongmen would blush to look.
Yes! thought the hapless cherub. *This has legs
and will one day be my ticket home.*

Jack in the Box

[*Léger mais fort*]

Jacques, a young entrepreneur, returns to Paris having made his fortune in the Texas oil fields. He has taken to wearing a ten-gallon hat and a pair of cowboy boots that make him appear taller than he is. He wastes no time in seeking out his favourite brothel in Montmartre and is greeted with enthusiasm by the heavy-breasted proprietress. *We have a young beauty, newly arrived from Provence, she says, one who smells of wild thyme and lavender. She too is well-travelled, mon brave, and may be yours for the night à bon prix.* He gladly pays the going rate and hastens up the stairs two steps at a time, the impact of his boots sending the hallway cats scurrying in all directions. Entering the scented room, he is awestruck by the vision before him, half-dressed, her warm smile capturing his heart and stiffening his resolve. *Ooh-la-la, Monsieur has a huge hat on,* she laughs, running an index finger down the buttons of his shirt to the top of his belt buckle. Then, flicking the brim of his hat with the same finger, she purrs, *Let me see, chéri, what I can do to get it off.* And while Jacques busily reaps the bounty of the southern regions, *la belle de Provence* walks in her mind from the bed to the window, from the window to the Seine, from the Seine to the ocean and the edge of the world and beyond to the last known galaxy where God sits alone, Her back to it all, thinking She should introduce Gabriel to enharmonic spellings and chronometric form, his horn playing lacking the depth of an expanding universe.

Petit prélude de "La Mort de Monsieur Mouche"

Primo

[*Ralentissez aimablement*]
The quartier was different back then, all hoodoo-voodoo and gangland romance. There were bokors everywhere flogging their painted dolls, and hit men with pencil moustaches and pomaded hair flirting with the skirts in the bars and cafés. The nightlife thrived and combos like ours made a killing. We played seven nights a week and drank for free. The women shimmied to our calypso stylings like we were a love drug. And they adored Jimmy, our front man, a Latino crooner with a satin voice and a velvet body, his charms conspicuous in the front of his white suit pants. Then one night Jimmy doesn't show up for the gig and he's found the next day in an alley, wearing a bullet hole like a red boutonniere. The tabloids took an interest in the murder for some reason and interviewed Jimmy's wife, a stripper from New Jersey who danced at a dive called Chicken Little's. *I loved da bum, I tell ya,* she reportedly said, *I truly did. Now he's sleepin' wit da angels. Alla dem, I'm sure, if ya catch my drift.* No one in the band even knew Jimmy was married. Anyway, we quit Paris after that and got a booking with a resort on the southern coast. It rained almost every night the whole time we were there, a steady downpour for an hour or so, cleansing and cooling – sorcerer's apprentice. But there was one night, I remember, not long after Jimmy's death, when the heavens were perfectly clear, and when we got up in the morning the beaches were littered with starfish. Hundreds and hundreds of astral bodies. As if the night sky had fallen.

Gris-gris

Secondo

[*Très terre-à-terre*]
Bead by bead, she whispers the promise of prayer,
her picture of salvation a holy card Virgin Mother

or angelic grandchild fading among the spilled phials
and ampoules. Crowded now onto the ground floor

of her three-storey walk-up, she lets the upper rooms
to penniless spinsters and widows, displaced colonials,

dreamless, their draped figures stiff in leather shoes
silhouetted at odd hours of the night descending

the staircase, disturbed by the scratch of wings outside
their walls, and uneasy with the incessant incantations,

the click-click-rattle, and finding all too often the front door
left unlatched, unlocked, an open invitation to the passing dark.

Véritables Préludes flasques (pour un chien)

[*La main en dessous*]
A widower stands and weeps at Bizet's grave
in the Cimetière du Père-Lachaise. It is the anniversary of Bizet's death.
Operatic passages coursing through his memory, he remains at the grave
for some time while other visitors come and go, paying him no notice.
Walking back to his apartment, he stops at a local *épicerie* to buy
a small bag of coffee and two squares of dark chocolate. On an impulse,
he buys one of several small containers of Chilean raspberries stacked neatly
on the counter. Outside his apartment building, he meets a neighbour
returning from walking New York, her miniature poodle. She is a widow,
attractive for her age, from America. He considers inviting her to join him
for coffee and perhaps to listen to *Carmen* or *Djamileh* but then thinks
her husband was probably the man who shot Liberty Valance and, *sans
doute*, she is the Chattanooga Choo Choo! Eyeing him and his purchases
as if she were scanning a well-worn libretto, she says, *You are right,
monsewer, to think I know nothing about the opera. But I can assure you,
I know a great deal about the raspberry.* Scooping up New York,
she smiles a parting *adieu* and enters the foyer picturing herself rounding third
as the Sultan of Swat to sweep the Yankees to their first World Series title.

Premier Menuet

Primus

[*Plus large*]

An Easter moon silenced her. Slit her tongue. Then her throat.
Or so we thought. But the dead have ways of telling their own story and
hers begins with news of the murder spreading fast across Paris, inter-
rupting the prayers of the faithful gathered in Notre-Dame for the Bishop's
vernal blessings. *Introibo ad altare Dei.* In the press rooms, the tabloid
editors pace their cages. Hungry for scandal, they spur on the paparazzi:
*Get off your asses, you skuzzbuckets! This isn't Palm Sunday. We have
deadlines!* In the courtroom, the accused sits pale in the prisoner's box,
caught lingering in the morning sky, purportedly plotting a diversionary
eclipse. The defence lawyers plead their client's innocence and parade
the dead girl's history of lunar worship and ritualistic practices. *Members
of the jury, it is our client who is the* real *victim here!* The prosecution
is perplexed. The evidence is inconclusive. *Dial M for moon, L for lunacy.*
In her chambers, the judge debates dismissing the case when unexpectedly
the *deus ex machina* of justice clanks into operation. *Fiat justitia, ruat
caelum.* An overlooked surveillance tape reveals a schoolgirl secreted
in the night shadows of the Roman shoreline outside the Temple to Jupiter,
the present-day site of Notre-Dame. She is waiting for the full moon
to balance perfectly on the tip of the cathedral spire, a mystical coupling
that she captures on film to share in private with her tittering roommates.
Then hurrying across the grounds to return to her dormitory in time
for curfew and evening prayer, she encounters the lions. *Dead lions and
martyrs*, she thinks, her mind igniting with the frenzy of a Roman circus,
and thrilling to the prospect of elephants.

Spirit travel

Secondus

[*Au pas*]
Backwards a goat to the Sabbat she rides,
To the Sabbat on a she-goat rides she.
Her leathery paps are wet with suckle,
The spewed suckle of the babe on her knee.

Behind her trail seven sallow-eyed hounds,
Seven sire hounds on legs spindle-narrow.
Should she tire, the babe will fall from her arms
And be devoured, flesh, bone, and marrow.

But the naked hag streams a pungent flow,
A serpentine flow she streams behind her
To bewitch the scent-crazed sallow-eyed hounds
And save the babe for the witching hour.

Amaryllis belladonna, naked lady, shades of night,
The Sabbat frees the sacrifice of the properties of light.

Où il est question du pardon des injures reçues

[*Que de monde!*]

It followed me from the cemetery. One of the many Montmartre cats
that appear and disappear between the gravestones. Little predators,
intimations of death itself. The groundskeepers warn that a simple
scratch from one of these beasts can create a festering wound.

Their caution crossed my mind as I crossed the street, my black dress
billowing in the wind. The cat followed, unmindful of the traffic.
When I reached the apartment building, it scooted through the entrance
and followed me up the stairs. I dashed ahead and managed to close
my apartment door just as it charged at the narrow opening. It thudded
against the bottom of the door frame reminding me of the time a year
earlier when my car was rear-ended at a stoplight. There were only
a few scratches. The other driver was apologetic and offered to pay
for repairs. A tall, handsome man, he phoned later that day to apologize
once again and to invite me to dinner. His *rrrr*'s purred as he spoke,
possibly some lingering trace of maternal accent or regional dialect.
But I suspected not, and graciously declined his invitation, closing
the door on any further advances.

Chasseur, et début de l'enterrement

ACT I

WHITE MOUSE: [*Wide-eyed*]
> OUCH! OUCH! OUCH! This tiresome cat's trying to eat me!

FEARSOME CAT: [*Relishing his advantage*]
> HEE! HEE! HEE!
> [*His amused expression changes abruptly to a sinister sneer.*]
> That's Fearsome Cat, rodent! And I'm e-RAT-icating vermin.

CHORUS: [*Hesitantly, unsure if they should intervene*]
> Everything . . . is . . . suspect.
> [*Fearsome Cat glares menacingly in their direction.*]
> Almost everything is suspect.
> [*They pause and stare at one another, uncertain*
> *of what to say next. Finally one of their members breaks*
> *the silence, awkwardly at first, but happy with the result.*]
> Even the . . . even the unsuspected!

ACT II

WHITE MOUSE: [*With trepidation*]
> OOH LA-LA! His claws are sharper than medicine balls.

FEARSOME CAT: [*Preening his whiskers with a forepaw*]
> My teeth too!
> [*Grins broadly, licking his incisors. His tongue, a brilliant pink.*]

CHORUS: [*Slowly, still uncertain of themselves*]
> Fearsome Cat is . . . posturing for political appointment.

[*They nod approvingly to one another, happy to direct the focus of attention away from the atrocity unfolding before them. Happy too to please Fearsome Cat.*]
Every op's a photo-op!
[*The FLASH! FLASH! of cameras as the curtain drops.*]

ACT III

FEARSOME CAT: [*Baiting the trap*]
Smile for the birdie!
[*Pounces on White Mouse.*]

WHITE MOUSE: [*With new-found ferocity*]
Say cheese first, villain!
[*Puts up a heroic fight.*]
Vive le fromage! Give me Liberté ™ or give me . . . .
[*Collapses and dies from scarlet bruising.*]

CHORUS: [*Again lost for words*]
Nothing detected . . . goes undetected.
[*They place White Mouse in a matchbox with the words **STRIKE HERE** printed on the side. Slowly, the stage fills with Seraphim attending the burial. Their prayers will heal the ills of the world.*]

EPILOGUE

[*The stage is empty as the curtain rises. The playwright enters from stage right, tearfully.*]
AIR-IKSATI:
You see, my most dear Biqui, there is a beginning to everything after all. A place to begin to be in.

[*Pause*]

Again.

[*Pause*]

I kiss you on the heart.

[FIN / RIDEAU]

TWO OPEN LETTERS

Prises d'air, jeux d'échecs et bateaux sur les toits

Primo

[*Très perdu*]
A chamber ensemble in formal black attire plays Mozart's Quintet
in A Major for clarinet, viola, two violins, and a cello. The musicians
are positioned along a sturdy wooden plank that is carefully balanced
on the top of an outcrop of barrier reef some distance from the shoreline.
A casual observer might easily think the five performers cormorants or
sooty terns were it not for the magnificence of their playing. A young girl
rows by the musicians in a dory. The determined expression on her tear-
stained face inspires their performance. Earlier that same day, she was
told by her grieving mother that her father had died during the night
from complications of a prolonged illness. A stranger to death, her plan
now is to row her sorrow far out to sea and drop it into the waves.
She remembers how once she watched through the fragrant wisteria
at the family's summer home as an uncle lowered a sack of newborn
kittens into a moonlit lake, breaking the spell of its mirrored surface.
Later that night, back in her attic bedroom, she dreamt she had drowned
trying to save the kittens. She knows now you never die in a dream.
At least, you don't *die* die, though you could die in your sleep and
never wake from the dream of waking from a dream.

Crime Passionnel: A Mystery in Five Parts

Secondo

[*Les 2 mains ensemble*]

1.

My dog found a finger in the park.
A long, slender finger. The kind that plays piano.
Next day she found an ear. Holding it to my ear
I heard the drowned strings of orchestras.
There were crows in the trees. I called the police.
We went to the park. My dog unearthed a voice.
When I picked it up, a song escaped.
Carried on the wind, it startled the crows.

2.

The inspector suspects foul play.
Wants to question my dog.
Wants to question me too.
Love me, I said, *love my dog.*
His eyes narrowed, studied me intently.
He was dusting for fingerprints.

3.

My dog has a talent for her new-found mission.
Uncanny but evidently not un-canine.
Even in the most inclement weather. Or at night.
Particularly at night. When there are shadows in the park.
And whispers. Choruses and choruses. Whispering.

4.
The inspector has assembled the findings.
The rib cage is too small to be human, he says.
Wouldn't fit a songbird, let alone a heart.
I said, *There are more species of songbirds*
in one square mile of Amazon rainforest
than in the rest of the entire world.
His eyes narrowed, fixed on mine.
He flipped open his notepad.
Drew a line through ~~crime passionnel~~.

5.
Today my dog found a heart.
A small, timid heart beating adagio,
the way a heart beats
when it has reason to hide itself
from those it loves.

Cheminées, ballons qui explosent

Primus

[*Sur la langue*]

As a babe in utero, she punched and kicked
at the walls of her mother's womb and her father, all but choked
with amazement and delight, would press his mouth to his wife's
protuberant belly and whisper, *What are you doing in there?*
She has no recollection of these moments, of course, yet
whenever she hears that question asked, she struggles to recall
the name or the face of some long ago playmate. Years go by
and her father, a healthy man by all appearances, suddenly dies
from an undetected ailment, leaving her feeling completely bereft.
She had dearly wanted him to live to hold his first grandchild.
Frustrated by his untimely death she presses her lips to his coffin
and grieves, *What are you doing in there?* Her weeping disturbs
the child she is carrying and it responds with kicks and punches,
a temperament that resonates *tic-toc* through her body
with the pendular swing of birth and death, the passage of time
a cuckoo's song.

Morning at the Museum with Mr. Rux

Secondus

[*Ne toussez pas*]
1.
If a train is travelling at the speed
of weather, and the weather is inclement,

how long will it take to reach the man
who broke the bank at Monte Carlo?

2.
The abacus beads at the Science **M**useum
are in coloured sets of ten. Red plus blue

plus green is. Green minus blue minus red
is. Or, possibly, is not.

3.
We are Mr. Rux's "Daycare of Demi-Einsteins"
or, as he proudly pronounces this morning,

"A Plethora of Pythagoreans!" preparing
to depart the Museum after our morning visit.

Walking back, "peripatetic, à la Aristotle,"
we come to a well-worn set of **RR** tracks,

the tracks for the morning train from Paris
to Lyon, en route to Monte Carlo.

4.

Crossing the tracks in single file, we hold tight
to a length of knotted rope and, once across,

Mr. Rux instructs, "Toddlers toggle, SVP,"
and our line divides. Now we walk parallel

in pairs – "A Coupling of Callippuses!" –
our rope forming a happy-faced **U**.

5.

Xing at traffic intersections is red, yellow,
green. Or red, orange, green.

Never cross on red because the word "cross"
also means angry. Walk on red and Mr. Rux

will come across very angry :-{{
– but à la Mr. Rux, his face changing

from mad to glad faster than a traffic light
or the morning train to Monte Carlo.

6.

We have dressed ourselves and only a few
of us have matching rain boots.

"Conformity is the ruin of genius!"
Mr. Rux exhorts, marvelling at us, his *protégés*.

7.

Back at the daycare, Mr. Rux and his wife kiss
hello – a convergence of parallel lines.

While we nap, Mrs. Rux prepares *un petit repas*,
and Mr. Rux, on the telephone, listens attentively

to the Museum custodian's recitation of articles
lost but newly found: four yellow rain hats,

three woollen scarves, two odd mittens –
rouge et noir – and one pocket calculator, kaput.

FURNITuRE MUSIC

Danses gothiques (Neuvaine pour le plus grand calme et la forte tranquillité de mon Âme)

[Cultifiement et coadunation choristique]

Amid tables, turned and overturned, scattered coins and feathered sacrifices, a gunman sits in a chair on the balcony of a hotel suite overlooking the Bourse de Paris. His temples are still pulsing from the exertion of his rage. He is on an assignment and has dressed in a navy blue suit, shirt and tie, black wingtips. The standard business attire of his occupation, conservatively chic. He tests the wind with a wetted finger, his trigger finger, calculating speed and trajectory, a compulsive habit, one of many. Pigeons are sunning on the window ledges that bookend the balcony. Their cooing murmur is meditative. It calms him. As his heart rate slows, he thinks, *We are many people before we become the person we are.*

Ce que dit la petite princesse des Tulipes

[*Ne changez pas de physionomie*]

A woman steps out of her bath and towels her skin dry,
reflecting on her body, how it has sustained the trials of love
and other crimes – money laundering, forgery, insider trading.
She stares into a full-length mirror and thinks aloud, *We are more*
than the sum of our blessings. She can be a desert wind but today
she is a cactus flower. She opens the window to let the steam vent
from the room, moves a potted azalea to the window ledge where
it will flourish in the morning sun. She remembers how once
she eclipsed that fiery ball while holding it to her lips. Her lips
did not blister and, for several nights thereafter, the sun stole back
to the place where she slept.

Gants de boxe et allumettes

[*Dans le creux de l'estomac*]

An American businessman, trader in currencies, exits the Banque Populaire in the financial district of Paris. He flags a passing taxi, but it is occupied and rushes by. He places his briefcase on the ledge of the bank's front window, lights a cigarette. He puts on sunglasses to shade his eyes from the noon sun and studies the window ledges of the facing apartment buildings. Wondering how many display potted azaleas, caged cockatoos, or burnt offerings, he taps ashes from the tip of his cigarette onto the pavement. Exhaling, he notices the wind has changed direction.

Choses vues à droite et à gauche (sans lunettes)

[*Continuez sans perdre connaissance*]

A taxi driver drops off a fare in front of the Banque Populaire
on Avenue d'Andorra. A woman of unusual beauty, she wears
the scent of desert flora. She pays with newly minted coins
and tips the driver handsomely. A man in sunglasses discards
his lit cigarette to help her from the car. She knows men,
all men, and so can read his desire but is distracted by a man
in a navy blue suit now entering the bank. She hurries to follow
behind him, leaving the taxi to the man in sunglasses. *Alors,
on va où, monsieur?* the cabbie asks, pious and pale as ash.
La Gare Montparnasse, s'il vous plaît. Detecting the American's
accent, the cabbie says, *Deserts speak to us of God's vast design
and infinite sorrow.* The man in sunglasses is still preoccupied
with the vision of the scented woman and does not respond.
They will arrive at the Gare Montparnasse before he realizes
that he has left his briefcase in the sunlight amid the pigeons
on the bank's front window ledge.

Dans laquelle les Pères de la Très Véritable et Très Sainte Église sont invoqués

[*Devenez pâle*]
A man in a navy blue suit and black wingtip shoes exchanges
pleasantries with an attractive bank teller. He withdraws a large sum
of money and places it in a leather portmanteau. He then enters
the bank manager's office, as if by appointment, and shoots him dead.
A silencer is used to muffle the shot and he leaves the bank unnoticed
by the security guards. No one but a woman, lightly scented with
the stamen powder of cactus flowers, witnesses the crime.
She is an accomplice in spirit, at one with widows and lepers,
and does not raise an alarm. The shooter deposits the gun in a briefcase
he finds on a window ledge outside the bank. He hails a cab and gets
into the back seat. The scented woman from the bank slides in beside
him. He does not know her but contains his surprise by focusing
on her beauty and a small scar on her upper lip. *In time, you could
begin to love me,* she whispers, her mouth close to his. *"Could"?*
he asks, his lips brushing hers as he forms his words, *You're not sure?*
Her eyes narrow, study the depth of his. *Everything is only possibility,*
she replies. *And with love there are multiplicities that extend to infinities,
numbers that would make a money-changer weep.* He likes the way
she thinks. *That suits me just fine,* he says. *It so happens I have
possibilities to kill.* She laughs, the tiny white fold of scar disappearing
in the full flush of smile.

MeDUSA'S TRaP

Le Porteur de grosses pierres

Primo

[*Seul, pendant un instant*]

It wasn't the year he lived under a large rock.
Nor was it the year he spent in a tree. No, it was just after I returned
to Paris from Tahiti, my study of the native dances of French Polynesia
finally complete. I went to visit him in the hospital where he was
being treated and we talked together all afternoon in the garden sitting
area. *The Tahitian women,* I told him, *have beautifully long limbs and
dance topless beneath the palm trees in bare feet. In bear feet?*
he responded sombrely. *How grizzly.* Yes, *très drôle* he was, a master
of the *bon mot.* He died later that night, the cause of death revealed only
to his immediate family, none of whom would speak to me. And there
was no funeral. Did I ever mention that he once walked across Paris
in a rare snowstorm to tell me that every word was once a poem? He did,
yes. Stood frozen in the doorway, a snowman. *Imagine the inspiration
for "abominable,"* he mused. Wouldn't even come in out of the cold.
My only visitor all winter.

After Charybdis

Secondo

[*De loin avec ennui*]
I've
come
apart
'Ive
come
undone
'
Ive
lost
the
art
of
Being
[one].

Après avoir obtenu la remise de ses fautes

[*Dans le dos*]

      The Falling Man fell four or five times a day. Bruising,
often bone-breaking falls that he could not seem to avoid no matter
how much he monitored his every step. His condition baffled doctors
and deeply disquieted his wife, who relied on him for everything.
She was the Floating Woman and by all estimates would now be
rounding Jupiter were it not for ceilings and the fact that she never
ventured outside. This made it necessary for her husband to attend
to all matters quotidian. Which he did, diligently. Until one day
he fell from a great height and died on impact. The news of his death
was delivered to his wife by the village vicar, an exceptionally tall,
lean man who afoot fittingly resembled a praying mantis. The vicar's
grave tidings sent the wife reeling into a state of shock and she flitted
frantically around the living room like an unknotted party balloon
before finally settling on the sofa, empty and deflated. She eventually
married the vicar and never floated again. This allowed her
to pursue her interest in playing the piano. The vicar's grand piano.
Or, as she preferred, *le piano à queue*. The piano with a tail.

Sur un arbre

Primo

[*Dans la tête*]

He was so familiar with the trees in the local park that when one spoke his name as he was passing he nodded *bonjour* in return as if acknowledging the greeting of a neighbour or casual acquaintance. It was only after he had walked on for several paces that he replayed the encounter in his mind. Even then he would not have given it much thought had the voice not sounded like her voice. He retraced his steps and stood in front of the tree as if to engage in conversation. Again the tree spoke, saying or rather singing his name with the same musical lilt of the remembered voice. He felt an urge to touch the tree, its smooth bark. But he resisted and, now feeling overly self-conscious, walked away. Had he thought to look up into the billowing branches he would have seen her, transformed, her beautiful yellow beak trilling his name in a song very like that of the warbling cuckoo.

Your Note

Secondo

[*Avec beaucoup de mal*]
It was chilling to watch you that morning
naked, searching through your suitcase for something clean to wear,
your arms as thin as the rails you'd ridden in on, blue-white
at the wrists, your flesh goosebumped. And later,
your compulsive spying through the grimy peephole,
as if anyone other than me would find you, trace the rusty stain
back into the washroom to where the hot water was still running
a pressureless, tepid trickle. Nothing in that fucking dump
of a hotel ever worked, and for the longest time after
I thought how it must have taken you forever
to learn such patience and craft so fine a calligraphy.

Profiter de ce qu'il a des cors aux pieds pour lui prendre son cerceau

Primo

[*En traînant les jambes*]

      A stealthy wind carries itself across the threshold and enters
the kitchen, disturbing curtains that have been drawn to block the sun,
the old sun, maleficent in its dotage, its solar flares singeing the wings
of homing pigeons, hampering the navigation of commercial airlines.
Princess Asphodel, with skin Saharan gold, stands silently in the open
doorway, unmindful of the wind but uncomfortably conscious of the sun.
Her posture bespeaks indecision, her temples pulsing to the stammer
of a common saw, *If you c-can't stand the heat g-get out get out.*
She moves to exit, but the wind catches the door, slams it shut.
The splintering sound enters her head sideways, like a dream or a blow
from some intruder, some smash-and-grab Jimmy, jumpy in his frog-
green balaclava. Startled, she staggers backwards into the kitchen,
colliding with wedding gifts still wrapped and boxed, relieved somehow
by a similarity in the sound of breaking stemware and broken spells.

Rewriting Silence

Secondo

[*Ne parlez pas*]
Old heat, this. Burnt and scaly dry.
And these hills? Old rock, give or take.
Once a gateway for migrant species,
the soil here is trodden, a timeless witness
      to af en
      eaf reen
      leaf green.
But it can't sustain us. Not all of us.
It needs time to recover from our ilk of ape.

So here, then, is my modest proposal:
let's you and I devolve arm in arm into being,
counter-clockwise to the drive of that primordial
gangbang we've come to lock loins with
and slide back on our bellies into the ocean's flesh,
the seminal quiet of our history, pulled by a force
more immense than moons or constellations,
and so far beyond our appetites, even for lust,
were we to parse its silent splendour
we might mistake it for poetry.

Cinq Grimaces pour "Le Songe d'une nuit d'été"

Primo

[*Au gré des flots*]

Cloudy, with intermittent showers. That was the weather forecast in Calais the morning he waded into the Channel to begin his solo swim around the world an unprecedented feat not that that entered his thoughts his mind a storm of the words he remembered spit wet on her lips their fury locked in the memory of his fingertips and transcribed into the music he composed after she'd gone the melodies screaming from his hands chased by village boys shouting *Shoo-shoo the Ugly Man* as they threw rocks and bottles his appearance having become frightful from the absinthe his reflection in the shop windows either too sharp or too flat he couldn't decide which wondering instead if breathing underwater is intuitive if salvation is a planet orbiting a star for billions of years without ever altering its course if the core of roiling magma under the earth's crust is a new world in the making as the universe evolves changing constantly like the weather that day in Calais cloudy with intermittent showers. The meteorologist had promised the next day would be clear and sunny, but, I mean, honestly, who among us really believes in promises anymore?

Cosmos Mariner

Secondo

[*Sans luisant*]
He waited anchored to his emptiness
      until weightless then freed
          upon a buoyant C

scaled the fixed-do solfège bel canto
      to wave to no one's *bon voyage!*
          and drift uncharted

between Scylla and Charybdis,
      his sails accordions
          folded luff to leech,

the whirling water not the blue deep
      of the eyes he remembered
          but fathoms deeper

than the breath he drew and held
      like the last note of a parting aria
          left suspended – *suspendu* –

before being engulfed by an ovation of waves
      and refracted starlight, *Goodnight, goodnight,*
          give my love to the World.

Lui manger sa tartine

Primo

[*Corpulentus*]
The morning she left him, she emptied a bottle of Givenchy perfume over the bedroom's porous floorboards. The perfume had been a gift from a painter for whom she often posed. Her husband had never liked its floral redolence, how it emanated from her slender body, and now he would have to live with it. Or more to the point, sleep with it.
It was a bold act on her part, meant to hurt and humiliate, although she was always one to assert she would never wish to make a lobster blush, or even an egg.

Hotel Genève

Secondo

[*Lent et triste*]
A written surrender, proclaimed and paraded
pipes and drums, aspiring to the condition of music,
revealing the abstract literature we'd become
in choosing to leave the sheets and blankets tangled
for the bed to reconstruct, or the chambermaid
to wonder at, her imagination inflamed by the scene
of capitulation, and the text of the armistice
you'd scrawled in lipstick across the dresser mirror,
a cursive severance of former alliances, lacking
syntax and abounding in clefs, commas, and codas,
the edits and erasures smearing the time signature
but leaving legible the final flourish of conditions
and territorial concession: ~~Icannotloveyou~~
~~Imustnotloveyou~~ *I have always loved you.*

La Danseuse et figures dans l'eau

[*Ne dormez pas, belle endormie*]
It is the Tournoi de Boules, Madame la Duchesse's annual fundraiser
for the Orphelinat Sainte-Cécile, and the Baronesse de Rêve-Roman
is a single point away from victory as she prepares to bowl her final ball.
A parasol opens in the crowd of hushed spectators. It belongs to
the Baronesse des Contes, rumoured to be the Baron de Rêve-Roman's lover.
The distraction breaks the crouching bowler's concentration at the critical
moment of release and she puts too much weight behind the ball causing it
to roll past its target to the very edge of the page, where it teeters before
tipping onto the reader's lap. Incensed, the Baronesse de Rêve-Roman,
a beautifully tall figure, flowering yet childless, stomps across the page
and halts before the white abyss of margin to glare at the reader, as might
a prominent-eyed Hamlet stand before a newly dug grave, indignant
at the gravedigger's industry. It is an awkward moment for the riveted
onlookers, with the exception, that is, of the Baronesse des Contes who is
casually folding her parasol, her movements the eclipsed genius of moon.

Petite Danse Finale (La Queue du Chien)

[*Enfouissez le son*]

A feverish student engaged in reading a French *roman* is speechless when the wooden sphere of a *boule* rolls from the paragraph he is perusing onto his lap. His surprise is heightened when next the *boule*'s proprietress, a baroness, famed for her beauty, turns her bewitching eyes on him, casting a look that bespeaks impatience and vexation. He gestures to return her cherished orb but his reach cannot penetrate the protective space of margin holding the text *suspendu. But how then,* he wonders, *did this little* o *of a thing manage to roll onto my lap? Quel imbécile!* the baroness exclaims, exasperated by the young scholar's ineptness. *Encore un Prince du Danemark!* Wildly gesturing her incredulity, she returns to her place in the story to regain the composure befitting her position. Meanwhile, from afar, a second baroness, she too of fabulous beauty, looks on with an interest perceptible to only the most attentive reader, her expression artfully masking her inner feelings, the slight curvature of lip a crescent moon rising, the slight bump of womb a turning tide.

Valse du "Mystérieux baiser dans l'oeil"

Primus

[*En plein vent*]
At night he flies. Short flights mostly, from rooftop to rooftop.
On moonlit nights, he perches atop the church steeple to view
the village's gentle slope down to the harbour. All this he keeps
to himself, not wanting the fuss and tumble of public attention.
However, his lack of spark throughout the morning hours
does not go unnoticed, and his friends and co-workers teasingly
accuse him of being a dark-eyed Don Juan. But teasing it is,
for everyone knows he loves only one and she cannot love him
back. So it is, so it must be. And so tonight, steeply perched,
he watches as the prevailing wind releases a swarm of luna
moths from the underside of the leaves in the church cemetery
and carries the swarm out to sea. There the moths are attracted
to the moon's reflection on the water and hover, a dark ellipse,
opening and closing above the waves like a mysterious portal
to a world underwater, inviting in the absence of sleep
or the flowering pale of asphodel.

~~Actias luna~~ A Congress for the Determination of the Directives and Defence of Illuminated Thinking

Secondus

[*Tremblez comme une feuille*]
~~Impulsive, the congress of luna moths~~
  ~~and the candle's radiant wick when already~~
   ~~each day entombs some hope or dream~~
~~forgotten or starred-crossed, like their wings~~
  ~~by design: the powdered pattern, a study in greens;~~
   ~~and, the motley moons, the gravedigger's genius.~~

  There is perhaps only distance after all,
or something remote and mathematical, in another day,
utterly still and quiescent, non-experiential.

  But that's fine, I have always been one for numbers.
(Last night I dreamed I had two willies! You can't imagine
how many things you can do with that thingamajig!)

  So just give me time
to put on a petticoat
  and then, dear Dog, I'm Yours,
   tendrement Vôtre,
    Yorick Satie

END MaTTER

AFTERWORD

The prose poems in this collection borrow titles from Erik Satie's piano compositions. Given that a number of Satie's piano works were written for four hands, the *primo* or *primus* voice of the prose poems is often accompanied by a *secondo* or *secondus* voice of poems written in other forms, traditional and contemporary. These do not take their titles from Satie. All of the poems are annotated in a manner similar to Satie's published piano scores, using a selection of his performance instructions, many of which, for example, "*comme un rossignol qui aurait mal aux dents*" (like a nightingale with a toothache), demonstrate Satie's attachment to the Paris Dada movement.

ACKNOWLEDGEMENTS

I have many people to thank for *Après Satie – For Two and Four Hands*. Critiques of some of the poems written before the idea for a collection had fully crystallized were provided by former writing group colleagues, including Rod Pederson, Roland Prevost, Rona Shaffran, Peter Richardson, David O'Meara, Adele Graf, and Norma Elliot. Master bricoleur, Stan Dragland, was first to read an early version of the collection and to provide detailed editorial input and assistance. I was also fortunate to have Beth Follett and Phil Hall read earlier versions of the collection and to benefit from their advice as gifted poets and editors. At Brick Books, I had the pleasure of working with the multi-talented Sue Chenette whose poetic insight and musicality helped, among other things, to shape the collection sequentially with all the shifts and progressions of a Satie piano score. And finally, the Brick production team of Alayna Munce, Marijke Friesen, Jessica Moore, David Seymour, and Kitty Lewis applied their many their skills and talents to the making of this wonderful-looking book. Thank you one and all. Thank you, thank you, thank you.

I have used Alan M. Gillmor's excellent biography, *Erik Satie* (Twayne Publishers, 1988), and Ornella Volta's thoughtful compilation of Satie's correspondence, *Satie Seen Through His Letters* (Marion Boyars, 1989) as references for those poems in the collection that relate directly to Satie and his relationship with Suzanne Valadon or to his association with the Paris Dadaists. The copy of Satie's piano score *Bonjour Biqui, Bonjour!* included here as a frontispiece can be found in Pierre-Daniel Templier's biography, *Erik Satie* (Paris, 1932, Plate xii). The image of the piano score is now in the public domain.

Three of the prose poems in the collection are ekphrastic responses to paintings by Munich artist, Quint Buchholz, whose works often focus on his devotion to books and reading.

Lastly, it should be noted that earlier versions of several poems in *Après Satie* were published in *Bywords Quarterly Journal, Descant, Sugar Mule, ottawater, Pith & Wry: Canadian Poetry* (Scrivener Press, 2010), and *Portrait w/tulips* (Leaf Editions, 2013). Their publication was very encouraging at the time, and I continue to be very grateful for this support.

DEAN STEADMAN's work has been published in Canadian journals and e-zines, as well as in the anthology *Pith & Wry: Canadian Poetry,* edited by Susan McMaster (Scrivener Press, 2010). He is the author of two chapbooks: *Portrait w/tulips* (Leaf Editions, 2013) and *Worm's Saving Day* (AngelHousePress, 2015). He was a finalist in the 2011 Ottawa Book Awards for his poetry collection, *their blue drowning* (Frog Hollow Press, 2010).